STUDY GUIDES

Mathematics

Year
5

Mark Patmore
and
Bob Hartman

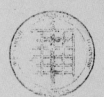

RISING STARS

Rising Stars UK Ltd, 22 Grafton Street, London W1S 4EX

www.risingstars-uk.com

Published 2007
Text, design and layout © Rising Stars UK Ltd.

Design: HL Studios
Illustrations: Oxford Designers and Illustrators
Editorial project management: Dodi Beardshaw
Editorial: Allison Toogood and Joanne Osborn
Cover design: Burville-Riley Design

British Library Cataloguing in Publication Data.
A CIP record for this book is available from the British Library.

ISBN: 978-1-84680-096-2

Printed by: Gutenberg Press, Malta

Contents

How to get the best out of this book

Most chapters spread across two pages but some spread over four pages. All chapters focus on one topic and should help you to keep 'On track' and to 'Aim higher'.

Title and **What will you learn?** tell you what you are aiming to learn.

Key facts: set out what you need to know and the ideas you need to understand fully.

Language: helps build up your mathematical vocabulary. Remember that some words mean one thing in everyday life and something more special in mathematics.

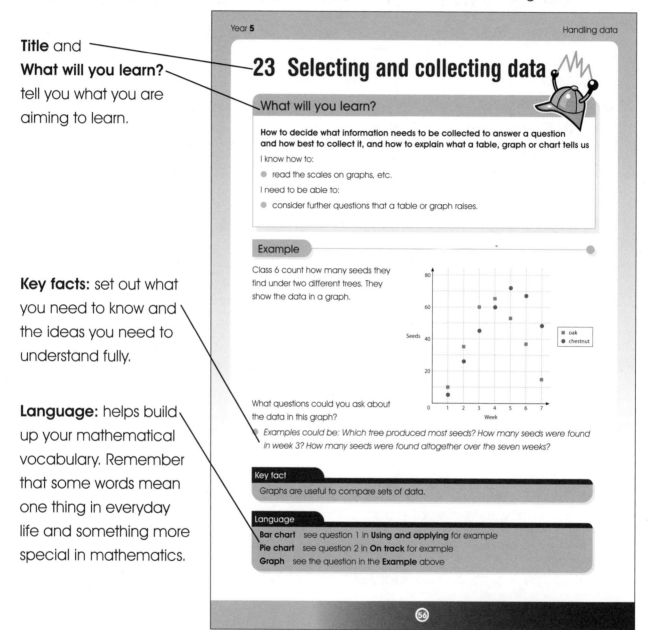

Follow these simple rules if you are using the book for revising.

1 Read each page carefully. Give yourself time to take in each idea.

2 Learn the key facts and ideas. If you need help ask your teacher or mum, dad or the adult who looks after you.

3 Concentrate on the things you find more difficult.

4 Only work for about 20 minutes or so at a time. Take a break and then do more work.

If you get most of the **On track** questions right then you know you are working at level 3 or 4. Well done – that's brilliant! If you get most of the **Aiming higher** questions right, you are working at the higher level 4 or 5. You're doing really well!

The **Using and applying** questions are often more challenging and ask you to explain your answers or think of different ways of answering. These questions will be around level 4 or above.

Some questions must be answered without using a calculator – look for 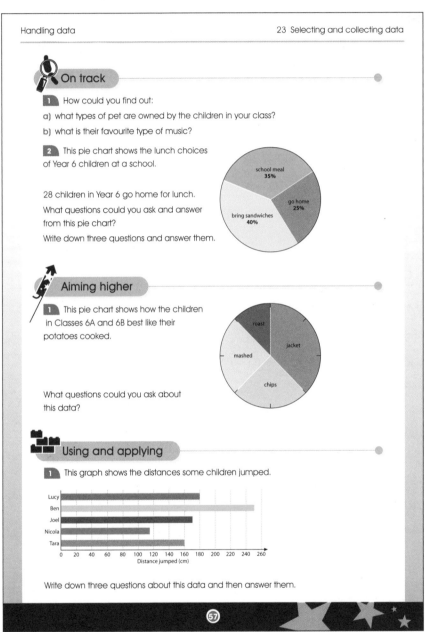. If you are not using a calculator be sure to write down the calculations you are doing. If you are using a calculator remember to try to check your answer to see if it is sensible.

Handling data   23 Selecting and collecting data

On track

1 How could you find out:
a) what types of pet are owned by the children in your class?
b) what is their favourite type of music?

2 This pie chart shows the lunch choices of Year 6 children at a school.

28 children in Year 6 go home for lunch.
What questions could you ask and answer from this pie chart?
Write down three questions and answer them.

school meal 35%
go home 25%
bring sandwiches 40%

Aiming higher

1 This pie chart shows how the children in Classes 6A and 6B best like their potatoes cooked.

roast
jacket
mashed
chips

What questions could you ask about this data?

Using and applying

1 This graph shows the distances some children jumped.

Lucy
Ben
Joel
Nicola
Tara

0 20 40 60 80 100 120 140 160 180 200 220 240 260
Distance jumped (cm)

Write down three questions about this data and then answer them.

57

Follow these simple rules if you want to know how well you are doing.

1 Work through the questions.

2 Keep a record of how well you do.

3 If you are working at level 3 or 4 you will get most of the **On track** questions correct.

4 If you are working at level 4 or 5 you will also get most of the **Aiming higher** questions correct.

1 Addition and subtraction with whole numbers and decimals

What will you learn?

How to count from any given number in whole-number and decimal steps, extending beyond zero when counting backwards

I know how to:

- relate numbers to their position on a number line
- find missing numbers in a sequence that includes negative numbers.

I need to be able to:

- solve addition and subtraction problems involving whole numbers.

Example

What is the next number in this sequence? 0.1, 0.3, 0.5, 0.7, 0.9

Here are four digit cards. Use three of the cards in the sum below to make a total as close to 1000 as you can.

| 2 | 3 | 7 | 4 |

574 + ☐ ☐ ☐

- *The numbers increase by 0.2 so the next number is 0.9 + 0.2, which is 1.1 (**not** 0.11).*
- *574 + 427 = 1001, which is nearest to 1000.*

Key facts

You can work out the difference between successive numbers in a sequence by subtracting the smaller from the larger, and checking with another pair of numbers. Remember that addition and subtraction are opposite operations. In the second example above, 1000 − 574 gives 426 so it is easy to see that 427 is the closest number possible to 426.

Language

Sequence   a set of numbers where there is a rule that states how the numbers increase or decrease

On track

1 What is the rule for this sequence? 5, 4.7, 4.4, ...

Suggest some other numbers that will be in the sequence.

2 Write the next three numbers in these counting sequences:

a) 7.7, 7.8, 7.9, ..., ..., ...   b) 2.5, 1.5, 0.5, ..., ..., ...

3 Write in the missing number on this number line.

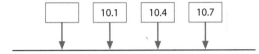

Aiming higher

1 Write in two numbers, each greater than 50, to complete this subtraction:

$$\square\square - \square\square = 37$$

2 Create a sequence that includes the number –3. Describe your sequence.

3 Write down the four numbers to make this subtraction correct:

```
  6  2  4  7
- □  □  □  □
-----------
  3  4  9  5
```

4 Write down the next two numbers of this sequence:

6.03, 6.02, 6.01, ..., ...

Using and applying

1 Here is part of a sequence: □, –9, –5, –1, □

Explain how to find the missing numbers.

2 Here is part of a sequence: 9, 8.7, 8.4, □, 7.8, 7.5, □

How can you find the missing numbers?

3 Explain how you would find the missing numbers in this sequence:

10, □, 4, 1, □, –5, □

What is the rule for the sequence?

2 Place value, rounding and ordering numbers

What will you learn?

What each digit represents in whole numbers and in decimals with up to two places

I know how to:

● partition, round and order these numbers.

I need to be able to:

● put numbers in size order.

Example

What is the value of the 7 in 64,105.73?

5070046 can be written as 5,000,000 + 70,000 + 40 + 6. Write 64,105.73 in the same way.

Round 17.46 and 19.58 to the nearest whole number.

● *You may find it helpful to put the number into columns as shown.*

Ten thousands	Thousands	Hundreds	Tens	Units		tenths	hundredths
6	4	1	0	5		7	3

The 7 is in the column of 'tenths' and so it represents seven tenths or 0.7.

● *60,000 + 4,000 + 100 +5 + 0.7 + 0.03.*

● *Look at the decimal part of each number. '46' is less than '50', i.e. less than half, so round down to 17. '58' is more than '50' so round up to 20.*

Key fact

The decimal point marks the separation between whole numbers and decimals.

Language

Value   the value of a digit is given by its position – how many hundreds or tenths, etc. it represents

On track

1 Copy and complete each of these:

a) $5017 = \boxed{} + 10 + 7$ b) $8\boxed{}7 = 800 + 40 + 7$

2 What decimal is equal to 37 hundredths?

3 Write the total of this calculation using decimals: $6 + \frac{3}{10} + \frac{7}{100} =$

4 Write a number in the box to make this correct:

$7.35 = 7 + 0.3 + \boxed{}$

Aiming higher

1 a) Write the value of the 5 in 21.57 as a fraction and then as a decimal.

b) (i) Write 21.57 rounded to the nearest whole number.
   (ii) Write 34.38 rounded to the nearest whole number.

2 Write these numbers using whole numbers and decimals (**not** fractions).

a) six thousand and twelve   b) nine-tenths

c) one and three-tenths   d) six, one-tenth and seven-hundredths

Using and applying

1 Write a decimal that contains seven units and five hundredths.

2 I started with a number and rounded it to the nearest whole number. The answer was 23. What number could I have started with?

3 Write a number that is bigger than 0.4 but smaller than 0.5.

4 Some children run a 100 m race on Sports Day. Here are their times in seconds.

Name	Time taken (seconds)
Tom	15.88
Harry	16.27
Emily	17.01
Callum	14.82
Jess	15.92

a) What is the winner's time?

b) Whose time is nearest to 16 seconds?

3 Fractions

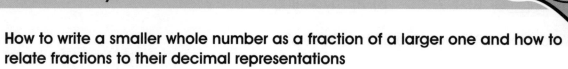

What will you learn?

How to write a smaller whole number as a fraction of a larger one and how to relate fractions to their decimal representations

I need to know how to:

- find equivalent fractions
- simplify fractions.

I need to be able to:

- multiply and divide numbers by, for example, 2, 3, 4 and 5.

Example

Write four-tenths as a decimal number.

What is three-quarters as a decimal?

One-quarter of a number is 8. What is the number?

- *Four-tenths* $= \dfrac{4}{10}$ $\qquad$ $\dfrac{1}{10} = 0.1$ so $\dfrac{4}{10} = 0.4$

- *Three-quarters* $= \dfrac{3}{4}$ $\qquad$ $\dfrac{1}{4} = 0.25$ so $\dfrac{3}{4} = 0.75$

- *One-quarter of a number is 8, i.e. $\dfrac{1}{4}$ of $\Box = 8$. (Note: This isn't asking you to find*

   $\dfrac{1}{4}$ *of 8.) Multiply by 4 to find a 'whole'. $4 \times 8 = 32$*

Key facts

A division can be written as a fraction and the phrase 'out of' is another way of expressing a fraction. For example, 3 out of 8 is written as $\dfrac{3}{8}$.

Equivalent fractions are found by multiplying or dividing the numerator and denominator by the same amount. Thus, multiplying both the 3 and the 8 by 2 shows that $\dfrac{3}{8} = \dfrac{6}{16}$.

Language

Numerator the top number of a fraction

Denominator the bottom number of a fraction

Equivalent means 'the same as'

Simplify means to find an equivalent fraction with the smallest denominator as possible

Proper a proper fraction is one where the numerator is less than the denominator

On track

1 Here is a chocolate bar.

Bill eats 5 pieces and Ann eats 3 pieces.

What fraction of the chocolate bar remains?

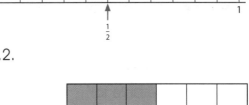

2 Mark $\frac{1}{4}$ and $\frac{5}{6}$ on this number line.

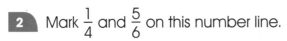

3 Write down two fractions that are the same as 0.2.

4 Which number represents the shaded
part of the figure?

a) 3.7   b) 0.25   c) 0.03   d) 7.3

Aiming higher

1 One-third of a number is 9. What is the number?

2 Find two different pairs of numbers to make this statement true: ☐ is $\frac{1}{4}$ of ☐

3 Here are two number cards.

One of the cards is 12.

The two number cards can make a fraction
equivalent to a quarter.

What two values could the second card be?

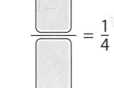
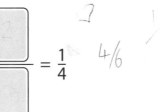

4 Amy has these number cards.

a) List all the fractions she can make choosing pairs of cards.

b) Write your fractions as proper fractions. Simplify the fractions if
you can.

c) Write your list in order of size, smallest fraction first.

Using and applying

1 What is the missing number?

$\frac{3}{10} = \frac{\square}{30}$ How do you know?

2 How could you show that $\frac{3}{12}$ is equivalent to $\frac{1}{4}$?

3 What fraction of £1 is 40p? Explain how you know.

4 Understanding percentages

What will you learn?

How to find simple percentages and that a percentage (per cent) is the number of parts in every 100

I know how to:

- multiply and divide by 10.

I need to be able to:

- express tenths and hundredths as percentages
- change percentages into fractions and decimals, and back into percentages.

Example

Shade 10% of this grid.

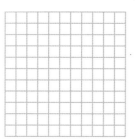 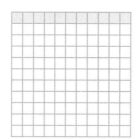

- There are 100 squares. Per cent means 'out of 100' so 10% is 10 out of 100 so 10 squares are shaded. 10% can be written as $\frac{10}{100} = \frac{1}{10}$.

Write these percentages as simplified fractions:

50%   6%   20%   30%   15%

- $50\% = \frac{50}{100} = \frac{1}{2}$ $6\% = \frac{6}{100} = \frac{3}{50}$ $20\% = \frac{20}{100} = \frac{1}{5}$ $30\% = \frac{30}{100} = \frac{3}{10}$

  $15\% = \frac{15}{100} = \frac{3}{20}$

Key fact

$1\% = \frac{1}{100}$ You can use this fact to work out other percentages as fractions.

Language

Percentage   means 'per cent' or 'per hundred' – think about 'century' meaning 100 years, or 100 runs in cricket

On track

1 **a)** Copy and shade 20% of this 8 × 5 grid.

b) Copy and shade 35% of this 10 × 10 grid.

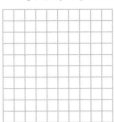

2 What is $\frac{45}{100}$ as a percentage?

3 What percentage of the bar is shaded?

4 A test has 50 marks. Rory gets 35 marks. What is his percentage score?

5 What percentage of this shape is shaded?

a) ▢   **b)** ◼   **c)** ▢

d) In another pattern using grey, black and white squares, 20% are grey, 40% are black. What percentage is white?

Aiming higher

1 45% of a class of children are boys. What percentage are girls?

2 Put these numbers in order, smallest first:

0.44   45% $\frac{4}{100}$ $\frac{4}{10}$

3 **a)** Write a **percentage** that is **greater than** $\frac{8}{10}$ and **less than** $\frac{90}{100}$.

b) Write a **decimal** that is **greater than** 25% and **less than** 50%.

c) Write a **decimal** that is **greater than** $\frac{1}{2}$ and **less than** 75%.

 Using and applying

1 Which is bigger: 65% or $\frac{3}{4}$? How do you know?

2 What percentage is the same as $\frac{8}{10}$? Explain how you know.

3 Which is a better mark in a test: 81% or 40 out of 50? How do you know?

4 Rick says that 4% is equivalent to $\frac{4}{10}$. Is he right? How do you know?

5 Solving problems involving proportion

What will you learn?

How to use sequences to scale numbers up or down, how to solve problems involving proportions of quantities, and how to continue a sequence such as:
There are 3 red sweets in every 10, there are 6 red sweets in every 20

I know how to:

- double and halve numbers.

I need to be able to:

- check my answers and see if they are sensible.

Example

John wants to make some bird tables to raise money for a wildlife charity.

He finds the following list of materials in a book.

> To make 3 bird tables you will need:
>
> 18 m of wood   3 wooden trays   48 nails

Write down what John will need to make 9 bird tables.

- *To make 9 bird tables everything in the list of materials must be multiplied by 3 so John will need 54 m of wood, 9 wooden trays and 144 nails.*

Key facts

The simplest way to solve problems is to find the value, or cost, of one thing – i.e. the cost of 1 pen – and then multiply by the new number of things.
Doubling and halving are useful techniques. If 200 g cost £1.80 how much do 150 g cost? Halve £1.80 to find the cost of 100 g (= 90p), halve again to find the cost of 50 g (= 45p) and then add together, so 150 g cost 135p or £1.35.

Language

Ratio   the name given to the process of comparing one part to another part. In a class of 30 children, if there are 20 boys and 10 girls, the ratio of boys to girls is 20 to 10 or 2 to 1

Proportion   the name given to the process of comparing one part to the whole. In this example, the proportion of boys in the class is 20 to 30 or 2 to 3

On track

1 18 is 6 times as many as 3.

What number is 6 times as many as 7?

2 a) Draw a diagram that shows this statement: 'My necklace has 3 yellow beads for every 4 green beads.'

b) Write a statement for this diagram.

3 Chocolate bars cost 45p each. How much would 7 bars cost?

Aiming higher

1 In St Hugh's school there are 20 girls and 30 boys in Year 5. Describe this with a sentence that uses the words 'for every'.

2 In a pattern for a bathroom, there is 1 white tile for every 3 pale grey tiles. How many white tiles are needed for 36 pale grey tiles and how many pale grey tiles are needed if there are 20 white tiles?

1 white
3 grey

2 white
6 grey

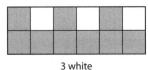

3 white
9 grey

Using and applying

1 In the 'Food from Germany' shop you earn one £1 voucher, to be spent next time, for every £15 you spend. How much must you spend to get 5 vouchers? Show how you worked this out.

2 A recipe gives amounts to feed 4 people. Show how you would change the amounts to feed 12 people.

2 eggs
110 g flour
110 g sugar
110 g butter

6 Place value

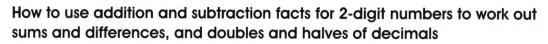

What will you learn?

How to use addition and subtraction facts for 2-digit numbers to work out sums and differences, and doubles and halves of decimals

I know how to:

● double and halve numbers.

I need to be able to:

● recognise that the place of a digit in a number shows the size of the number.

Example

Double 37. Use your answer to find double 0.37. What is the relationship between the two calculations?

● *37 × 2 = 74*

0.37 is one-hundredth of 37 so 0.37 × 2 will be 0.74, i.e. one-hundredth of 74.

12 + 34 = 46. Using the same digits in the same order how would you write an addition sum to give the answer 0.46?

● *0.12 + 0.34 = 0.46*

Key fact

The place of a digit in a number shows the size of the number. For example:

Hundreds	Tens	Units	tenths	hundredths	
	6	8	1	2	$= 60 + 8 + \dfrac{1}{10} + \dfrac{2}{100} = 68.12$
6	8	1	2		$= 600 + 80 + 1 + \dfrac{2}{10} = 681.2$

Language

Relationship means the 'connection' or 'link' between numbers

On track

1 Find half of 78. Use your answer to find half of 0.78. What is the relationship between the two calculations?

2 What number added to 0.78 gives 1? Show how you would check this.

3 What numbers should be written in the boxes to make these calculations correct?

a) $275 = 200 + \boxed{} + 5$

b) $60 + \boxed{} + \boxed{} = 64.9$

c) one half of $\boxed{} + \boxed{} = 4.3$

4 I think of a number, double it and get 5.4. What was my number?

Aiming higher

1 $30 \times 1.7 = 51$. Without using a calculator, write down the answer to $\underline{15} \times 1.7$.

2 Choose the two numbers in the following list that sum to 1.

0.26   0.8   0.84   0.74   0.02

Now write down the sum if each of these two numbers is divided by 2.

3 $2.4 - 1.7 = 0.7$. Write down two other decimal numbers with a difference of 0.7.

4 Double 4.2 gives the same answer as $10 - \boxed{}$. What number should I write in the box?

Using and applying

1 What number lies exactly halfway between 0.34 and 0.78? Show how you worked this out.

2 I think of a number, halve it, then add 0.4. I get the answer 7.2. What number did I start with? Show how you worked this out.

3 Complete the following by writing down what numbers should be in each box:

a) one half of $\boxed{}$ is the same as double $\boxed{}$ and is equal to 26

b) one half of $\boxed{}$ is the same as double $\boxed{}$ and is equal to 4.8

7 Multiplication

What will you learn?

How to use the multiplication facts up to 10 × 10 to multiply pairs of multiples of 10 and 100

I know how to:

● multiply and divide by 100.

I need to be able to:

● recognise that multiplication and division are inverse operations.

Example

Given that 3 × 240 = 720, write the answers to: 30 × 24, 300 × 24, 30 × 240

Now write down any division facts you can using these numbers.

● *30 × 24 = 720, 300 × 24= 7200, 30 × 240 = 7200*

● *For example: 720 ÷ 30 =24, 720 ÷ 24 = 30; 720 ÷ 3 = 240; 7200 ÷ 3 = 2400*

Write down the answer to four times three.

Now write down the answer to forty times thirty times ten.

● *4 × 3 = 12*

  40 × 30 × 10 = 12,000

Key facts

Multiplication and division are inverse, that is, opposite operations.
For example, 4 × 3 = 12 so 12 ÷ 4 = 3

Language

Product   means the answer to a multiplication calculation. For example, the product of 4 and 3 is 12 because 4 × 3 = 12

On track

1 **a)** How many eights are there in 56?   **b)** Divide 60 by 3.

c) Divide 240 by 4.

2 Write in the missing numbers.

a) $4 \times 80 = \square$ **b)** $500 \times 5 = \square$ **c)** $4 \times \square = 320$

3 **a)** What is 50 x 70?

b) Six times a number is 300. What is the number?

c) How many sevens are there in 420?

d) A number multiplied by itself gives 1600. What is the number?

4 What could the missing numbers be?

$\square \times \square = 120$

Now write down what the missing numbers could be for $\square \times \square = 1200$

Aiming higher

1 Using what you know about 36, how many multiplication and division facts can you make? How did you work out the division facts?

2 Find two numbers with a product of 1,500. What other pairs can you find?

3 Find five different ways of completing this calculation:

$360 \div \square = \square$

4 20 × 30 is the same as 40 × 15. What do you notice about the pairs of numbers?

Now write down a pair of numbers that multiply to give the same answer as: 50 × 30.

Using and applying

1 The product is 400. At least one of the numbers is a multiple of 10. What two numbers could have been multiplied together? Are there any other possibilities?

2 How many times bigger is 1800 than 6? How do you know?

3 What is 1800 ÷ 20? Explain how you know.

4 Make up some division questions that have a remainder of 1. How did you do it?

8 Factors and multiples

What will you learn?

How to find common multiples and how to identify pairs of factors of 2-digit whole numbers

I know how to:

- multiply and divide by numbers up to 100.

I need to be able to:

- recognise factors and multiples.

Example

Here are six number cards.

Which two numbers on the cards are factors of 42?

Which numbers on the cards are multiples of 4?

Now write down two common multiples of 4 and 12. These numbers will not be on the cards.

- *3 and 7*
- *12 and 28*
- *Common multiples are numbers that are in the 4 and 12 times tables so 24, 36, 48 are common multiples.*

Key fact

A factor of a number is smaller than the number; a multiple of a number is larger than the number – it is easy to forget which is which.

Language

Factor   the factors of a number are those numbers that divide exactly into the number. For example, the factors of 30 are 1, 2, 3, 5, 6, 10, 15, 30

Multiple   the number you get from other numbers by multiplication. For example, $77 = 7 \times 11$; 77 is a multiple of 7 and a multiple of 11. Multiples are in a number's times table

On track

1 Which of the following numbers are factors of 48?

2, 3, 4, 6, 8, 10, 12, 14, 16, 18, 20

2 Show how you would use factors to:

a) multiply 18 by 15.   b) divide 108 by 12.

Aiming higher

1 Lucy and John are playing a game with a set of cards. Each card has a number between 1 and 36 on it. Lucy takes a card and John has to work out what number is on her card using the following facts that Lucy gives him:

● 3 is a factor of the number

● the sum of the digits in the number lies between 4 and 8

● it is an odd number

● when the digits are multiplied together the total lies between 4 and 8.

What is the number on Lucy's card?

2 Find two numbers that have exactly four factors including 1.

3 Two numbers are in the wrong place in this sorting diagram.

Which two numbers are they? Copy the diagram with the numbers in the correct place.

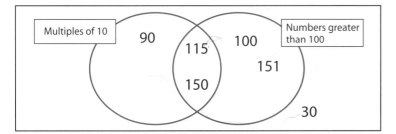

 Using and applying

1 The area of a rectangle is 24 cm². What are the lengths of the sides? How many different answers can you find?

2 Write down four different square numbers. How many different factors does each square number have? What do you notice? Now check with another square number.

3 Write down three common multiples for 4, 6 and 8. How did you find them?

9 Estimating and checking

What will you learn?

How to estimate and check the result of a calculation

I know how to:

● round numbers and measurements to the nearest whole number or measure.

I need to be able to:

● check answers by doing the opposite (inverse) calculation.

Example

A ruler and two pencils cost 40p.

Two rulers and five pencils cost 85p.

How much is one pencil?

Check that your answer fits the problem.

Four friends share £7900 equally. Roughly how much is this for each person?

● *1 ruler and 2 pencils cost 40p so 2 rulers and 4 pencils will cost 80p, but 2 rulers and 5 pencils cost 85p so 1 pencil costs 5p.*

   Checking: Therefore 2 pencils cost 10p so 1 ruler costs 30p, and 2 rulers and 5 pencils cost (2 × 30p) + (5 × 5p) = 85p.

● *Round £7900 up to £8000. Dividing £8000 by 4 gives £2000.*

Key facts

When rounding, using a number line, move to the right if the last number is 5 or more; move to the left if the last number is less than 5. For example, 137 cm to the nearest metre is 1 m, but 157 cm to the nearest metre is 2 m.
Check answers by doing the opposite calculation – divide instead of multiply – or by using approximate rounded values.
Always try to think what the rough answer will be – see the second **Example** question.

Language

Roughly, approximately   these are words used to mean the same as 'around' – the exact answer isn't required, only an approximate answer

On track

1. Which is the closest estimate for 2345 + 5678?

a) 6000   b) 6300   c) 7000   d) 7300

Show how you worked out your estimate.

2. Estimate the answer to 5678 − 2345.

3. 17,895 men and 16,243 women attended a football match. Roughly, how many people attended altogether?

4. Write down a multiplication problem that will have an answer close to 1500. Check your answer using division.

Aiming higher

1. Round these measurements to the nearest whole unit:

a) 43.75 cm   b) 4.56 km   c) 1.86 kg

2. What is the approximate perimeter of this hexagon?

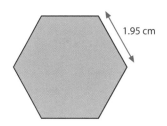

1.95 cm

3. What is the approximate area of this rectangle?

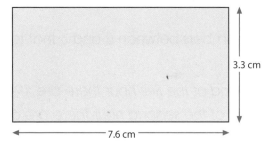

3.3 cm

7.6 cm

Using and applying

1. There are about 80 potatoes in a 10 kg bag.

A large restaurant uses about 2 potatoes per portion of chips.

They charge £1 for a portion of chips.

Estimate how much money the restaurant takes for chips on a day that they use 100 kg of potatoes.

2. Here are some problems with a choice of answers. Without working out the exact answer, select the answer you think is most reasonable and write down the rough calculation that you did.

a) Four video recorders cost £812 so the cost of one recorder is:

(i) £23   (ii) £40   (iii) £230   (iv) £400

b) Find the cost of 31 CDs at £8.50 each.

(i) £130   (ii) £260   (iii) £390   (iv) £520

10 Written methods of calculation 1

What will you learn?

How to use efficient written methods to add and subtract whole numbers and decimals with up to two places

I know how to:

● change units, i.e. change kilograms into grams.

I need to be able to:

● explain each step in addition and subtraction calculations.

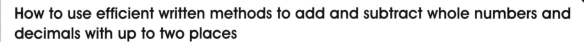

Example

A new record shop opened.

During the first hour, 194 people came in and 127 people left.

During the second hour, 78 people came in and 93 people left.

How many people were still in the store after two hours?

Find two numbers between 2 and 3 that total 6.4. Show how you check your answer.

● *At the end of the first hour there are 194 – 127 people in the shop = 67 people. At the end of the second hour there are 67 + 78 – 93 people = 52 people.*

● *Because 2 + 3 = 5 the decimal part of both numbers must be greater than 5 in order to give a 'carry' of 1 when they are added. So possible answers are: 2.6 + 3.8 or 2.8 + 3.6 or 2.7 + 3.7 ...*

Key facts

Line up decimal points and make sure numbers are always lined up correctly when setting out addition and subtraction calculations.
Take care with units. For example, always work in grams or kilograms not in a mixture of both.

Language

Total means 'sum' – the answer to an addition calculation
Difference in this context, difference means the answer to a subtraction calculation

On track

1 Work out 4563 – 1647, explaining every step that you write.

2 Find two numbers between 4 and 5 that total 9.68. Use a written method to check your answer.

3 Three parcels weigh 995 g, 65 g and 0.35 kg. How much do they weigh altogether?

4 I had 0.8 kg of sugar. I have 520 g left after I make a cake. How much sugar did I use?

5 Max jumped 10.45 m on his second try at the triple jump. This was 98 cm longer than on his first try. How far in metres did he jump on his first try?

Aiming higher

1 Jen is exploring the depth of a swimming pool.

She uses a 9 m-long pole. When the pole touches the bottom of the pool, twice as much of the pole is sticking out of the water as is in the water.

How deep is the water in the pool?

2 In the first year a raffle sold 1572 tickets, in the second year it sold 1753 tickets, and in the third year it sold 152 less than in the second year.

How many raffle tickets were sold in total over the three years?

Using and applying

1 Two numbers have a difference of 1.58. One of the numbers is 4.72. What is the other? Is this the only answer?

2 What are the missing digits in this calculation?

$$4\ \square\ 6\ 7$$
$$-\ 2\ 8\ 4\ \square$$
$$\overline{1\ 7\ 1\ 8}$$

Explain your reasoning.

3 What could the two missing digits be?

$\square 73 + \square 85 = 1058$

4 Brian is mixing some paints to make a pale green paint. He mixes 2.5 l of red paint with 0.85 l of yellow paint and adds 670 ml of white paint. How much paint does he make?

11 Multiplying and dividing by 10, 100 and 1000

What will you learn?

How to multiply and divide whole numbers and decimals by 10, 100 or 1000

I know how to:

● check answers.

I need to be able to:

● use a calculator efficiently.

Example

Find the missing numbers without using a calculator:

$39 \times ? = 390$ $6000 \div ? = 60$ $500 = ? \div 10$

● *10 – the 3 in the tens column has moved into the hundreds column.*

● *100 – the 6 in the thousands column has moved into the tens column.*

● *5000 – the 5 in the hundreds column must have been moved from the thousands column when divided by 10.*

Key facts

	Hundreds	Tens	Units	tenths	hundredths	thousandths
		6	8	1	2	
× 10	6	8	1	2		
		6	8	1	2	
÷ 10			6	8	1	2

Multiplying by 10 moves digits one column to the left.
Dividing by 10 moves digits one column to the right.

Language

Tenths (t) $\frac{1}{10}$ of a unit

Hundredths (h) $\frac{1}{100}$ of a unit

On track

1 How many tens are there in one thousand?

2 Divide 8400 by 100.

3 Write in the missing number: $5600 \div \boxed{} = 100$

4 Write what the four missing digits could be: $\boxed{}\boxed{}\boxed{} \div 10 = 3\boxed{}.\boxed{}$

5 Divide 101.1 by 10.

Aiming higher

1 **a)** How many times larger than 40 is 4000?

b) How many times smaller than 400 is 4?

2 A single operation on a calculator could be '× 10', '× 100' or '÷ 10', etc.

Here are some pairs of numbers. Write down what single operation you would do on your calculator to change the first number into the second number.

a) 4367, 43.67   **b)** 7.49, 749.0   **c)** 1001, 100,100   **d)** 5.6, 0.056

3 What numbers should I write in the boxes?

a) $3400 \div \boxed{} = 100$ **b)** $1700 \div \boxed{} = 170$

Using and applying

1 I divide a number by 10, and then again by 10. The answer is 0.8. What number did I start with? How can you check?

2 What number is ten times as big as 0.03? How do you know that it is ten times 0.03?

3 What numbers should I write in the boxes?

a) $6800 \div 6800 = \boxed{}$

b) $6800 \div 680 = \boxed{}$

c) $6800 \div 68 = \boxed{}$

What do you notice about the answers?

Use what you have noticed to write down the answer to $6800 \div 6.8$

12 Written methods of calculation 2

What will you learn?

How to calculate answers to questions like: 345 × 6; 34 × 56; 3.4 × 5; 345 ÷ 6

I know how to:

- round answers up or down.

I need to be able to:

- estimate the results of calculations.

Example

There are 14 packets of biscuits in a box. A school buys 24 boxes. How many packets does the school buy?

You need to calculate 14 × 24.

×	**10**	**4**
20	200	80
4	40	16

Total = 200 + 80 + 40 + 16 = 336

Key facts

Set out calculations as larger number × smaller number.

Language

Total   means the answer to an addition

Remainder   the fraction that is left when doing a division

 **On track**

1   There are 270 seats in Theatre 1 and 150 more seats in Theatre 2 than in Theatre 1.

a) How many seats are there in Theatre 2?

Both theatres are open from Wednesday to Saturday. One week both theatres are full each day they are open.

b) How many people went to shows at the theatres that week?

2 Write in the missing digits to make this correct.

$$
\begin{array}{r}
\boxed{}\,5\,\boxed{} \\
\times \qquad 7 \\
\hline
1\ 7\ 9\ 2
\end{array}
$$

3 I have 7 parcels each weighing 149 g. How much do they weigh altogether?

4 36 boxes of dog food weigh 38 kg each. How much do they weigh altogether?

5 I fill 5 jugs with water. Each jug holds 2.2 l. How much water do I have altogether?

Aiming higher

1 261 children and 27 teachers go on a coach trip.
How many 49-seater coaches will the school need to hire?

2 Maria and her sister want to buy a present for their mother.

Maria has £17. Her sister has double that amount.

They want to buy their mother a coat that costs £60.

How much more money do they need?

3 Carpet tiles are sold in boxes of 10 tiles.

Amy needs 123 carpet tiles.

How many boxes should she buy?

How many tiles will she have left over?

Using and applying

1 What is the total mass of 565 screws each weighing 9 g?

Show how you can estimate the answer.

2 Find a number between 450 and 460 that gives a remainder of 5 when divided by 8. How did you find the number?

13 Finding fractions and percentages

What will you learn?

How to find fractions of numbers using division, for example, to find $\frac{1}{3}$ of a number by dividing it by 3, and how to find a simple percentage of a quantity

I know how to:

- double and halve numbers.

I need to be able to:

- change a percentage into a fraction
- divide numbers by less than 10.

Example

One-quarter of a number is 8. What is the number?

Find 75% of 1 kg.

- *This question is asking what number, divided by 4, has 8 as the answer. Remembering that multiplication and division are reverse operations, multiply 8 by 4, giving 32.*
- *Change the kilogram into grams, giving 1000 g. 50% of 1000 g = 500 g. Therefore, 25% = 250 g. Thus 75% = 500 g + 250 g = 750 g.*

Find 5% of £480.

- *10% is the same as $\frac{10}{100}$ which equals $\frac{1}{10}$. So find one tenth of £480 = £48 5% is half of 10% so 5% of £480 = £24.*

Key fact

Use easy fractions or percentages, such as 50%, and then double or halve, etc. to make calculations easy.

Language

Unit fractions   fractions whose numerator is 1. $\frac{1}{10}$ is a unit fraction

Percentage   means 'per hundred' – look back at Unit 4

On track

1 **a)** One-fifth of a number is 10. What is the number?

b) One-seventh of a number is 8. What is the number?

2 Write down the calculation you would do to find $\frac{1}{8}$ of 256 and then write down the answer.

3 What is two-thirds of 66?

Aiming higher

1 Find 75% of 360 ml.

2 Which is greater: $\frac{3}{5}$ of 60 or 50% of 58?

3 To find 17.5% of 360 Kate does the following calculation:

10% of £360 = $\frac{1}{10}$ of = £36

5% of 360 = $\frac{1}{2}$ of 10% = £18

2.5 of 360 = $\frac{1}{2}$ of 5% = £9

so 17.5% of £360 = £63

Use this method to find 17.5% of £600.

4 John had £10. He gave 25% to a charity. How much did he have left?

Using and applying

1 Using letters, write out the names for the numbers from 1 to 10.

What percentage of the numbers have three-letter words?

What percentage of the numbers have four-letter words?

2 Find two different ways to fill in the gaps in this statement:

... % of ... = 30

3 Three-quarters of a number is 48. What is the number?

How did you work it out?

14 Properties of shapes

What will you learn?

How to recognise features of shapes such as rectangles, triangles and cubes, draw nets of cubes, recognise line symmetry and parallel and perpendicular sides

I know how to:

● draw and measure lines accurately.

I need to be able to:

● use the language of shapes correctly, e.g. 'face', 'vertex' and 'right angle'.

Example

This is a regular octagon. Its sides are labelled a, b, c, d, e, f, g and h.

Which side is parallel to side a?

Side g is perpendicular to side a. Which other side is also perpendicular to side a?

How many pairs of parallel sides are there in the octagon?

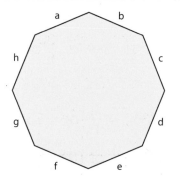

● e   ● c   ● *4: a, e; b, f; c, g; d, h*

Key facts

This is a **cube**.

This is a **rectangle**.

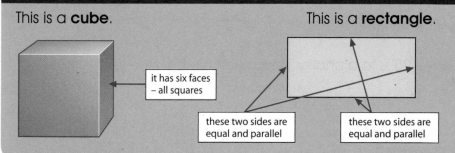

it has six faces – all squares

these two sides are equal and parallel

these two sides are equal and parallel

Language

Equilateral triangles   all three sides are the same length

Isosceles triangles   two sides are the same length

Scalene triangle   all three sides are different in length

Face   a flat side

Vertex (plural **vertices**)   a corner

Edge   the line joining two vertices, the boundary between two faces

On track

1   Here is part of a shape on a square grid. Copy on squared paper and draw three more lines to make a shape that has a line of symmetry.

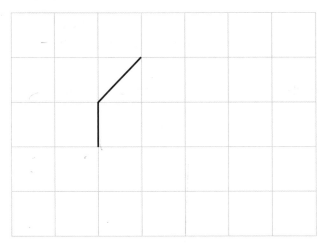

2   Add three more squares to complete this net of an open cube.

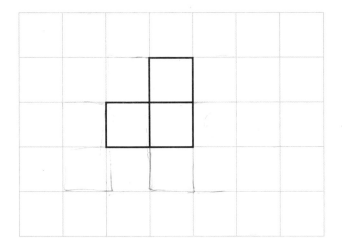

3   Triangle A has sides 10 cm, 12 cm, 6 cm. S

Triangle B has sides 8 cm, 10 cm, 8 cm. I

Triangle C has sides 20 cm, 30 cm, 20 cm. I

Triangle D has sides 6 cm, 6 cm, 6 cm. E

Which triangles are:

a) scalene

b) isosceles

c) equilateral?

4 **a)** Match each shape to the correct description in the table.

  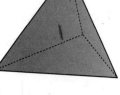 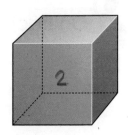

| A | B | C | D |

Shape letter	Number of vertices	Number of faces	Number of edges
	4	4 8	6
	8	6 14	12
	6	8 14	12
	5	5 10	8

b) For each shape, add the number of vertices and the number of faces together. What do you notice?

5 Copy and complete each sentence with the name of the correct triangle.

● In an _____ triangle all three sides are equal in length and all three angles are equal in size.

● An _____ triangle has only two equal sides and two equal angles.

● In a _____ triangle no two sides or angles are equal.

● In a _____ triangle one of the angles is a right angle.

Aiming higher

1 Here is a regular octagon. Join three of the dots to make an isosceles triangle. Use a ruler.

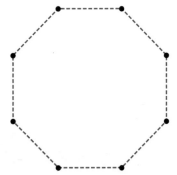

Join three dots to make a different isosceles triangle.

Now join three dots to make a right-angled triangle.

Join three dots to make a scalene triangle.

2 This is a drawing of a triangular prism.

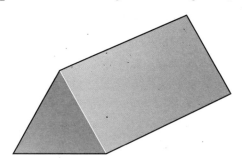

a) Which of these drawings are nets for the triangular prism?

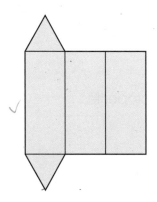

A

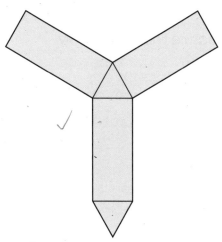

B

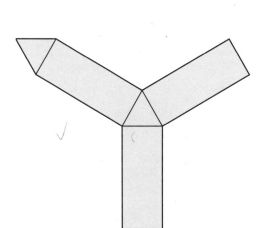

C

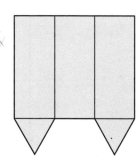

D

b) How many vertices does the triangular prism have?

Using and applying

1 Is this a net for an open cube? Explain why not.

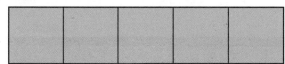

2 Is it possible for a quadrilateral to have exactly three right angles? Why not?

15 Using co-ordinates and drawing shapes

What will you learn?

How to read and plot co-ordinates in the first quadrant, how to use a set square and ruler to draw shapes with perpendicular or parallel sides

I know how to:

● draw and measure lines accurately.

I need to be able to:

● recognise simple 2D shapes and know facts about their properties.

Example

(3, 1) and (6, 5) are two vertices of a right-angled triangle. What are the co-ordinates of the third vertex? Are there any other possibilities?

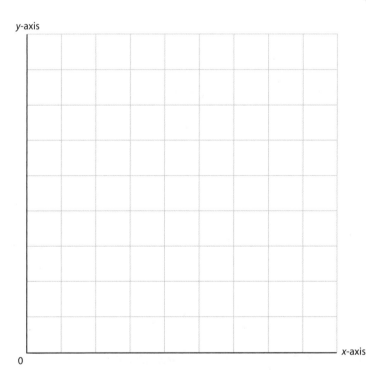

● *Possible co-ordinates are (6, 1) and (3, 5).*

Key fact

Co-ordinates are used to give positions on a grid. A co-ordinate has two numbers: the first number is the distance across the grid; the second number is the distance up the grid.

Language

Perpendicular   another way of saying at right angles or vertical

Vertex (plural **vertices**)   a corner. A triangle has three vertices

On track

1

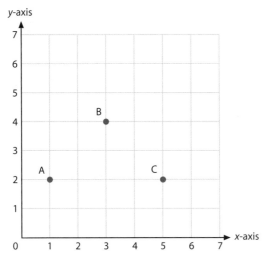

A, B and C are three corners of a square. Write down the co-ordinates of the other corner.

2 Draw a line like this across the page.

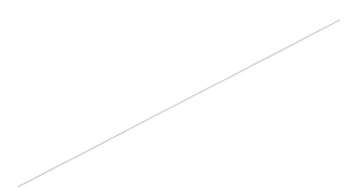

Now use a set square and ruler to draw a line parallel to your line.

3 The coordinates of a square are (3, 11), (8, 11), (8,6) and (3, 6).

The point (5, 8) is inside the square. Write down the coordinates of another point which is inside the square.

Aiming higher

1

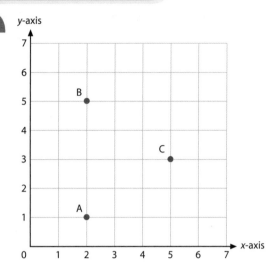

A, B and C are the vertices of an isosceles triangle.

Write down the co-ordinates of another point P, which would make A, B and P the vertices of a right-angled isosceles triangle.

2 Copy the grid below and mark the point (3, 4). Measure its distance from the origin.

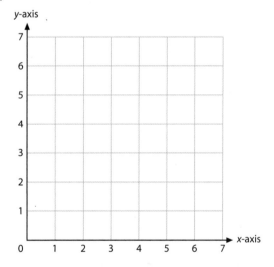

3 On a grid, mark the point (1, 2) and label it A.

On the same grid, mark the point (5, 4) and label it B.

Join A and B to make a straight line.

Draw another line parallel to this line. Label the ends of this line P and Q.

Write down the co-ordinates of P and Q.

Using and applying

1 For the points of the straight line on the grid, copy and complete the table below.

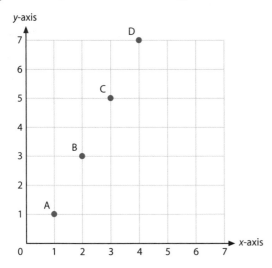

Point	Co-ordinates
A	(1, 1)
B	
C	
D	(4, 7)

Look carefully at the table.

Write down what you think are the co-ordinates of the next 3 points, E, F and G.

How did you work them out?

2 Amy is asked to draw a triangle with corners at (6, 4), (1, 3) and (3, 1).

This is what she drew.

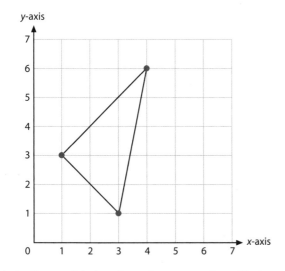

Explain the mistake Amy has made with her co-ordinates.

What sort of triangle has she drawn?

16 Symmetry, reflection and translation

What will you learn?

How to complete patterns with up to two lines of symmetry and how to draw the position of a shape after a reflection or translation

I know how to:

- draw and measure lines accurately.

I need to be able to:

- use co-ordinates in the first quadrant

- recognise shapes with line symmetry.

Example

Write down the co-ordinates of the triangle after reflection in the mirror line.

Write down the co-ordinates of the triangle after it has been translated 5 units to the right, parallel to the x-axis, and 2 units up, parallel to the mirror line.

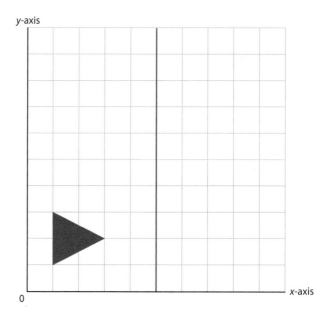

- (7, 2), (9, 1), (9, 3)
- (6, 3), (6, 5), (8, 4)

Key facts

Give a translation with the distance moved up or down or left or right.
A reflected shape is 'flipped over' so that it is the same distance from but on the opposite side of the mirror line as the original shape.

Language

Symmetry/symmetrical   a shape has (line) symmetry if it is the same on either side of a mirror line

 On track

1 The heavy lines are lines of symmetry. Copy and complete the pattern.

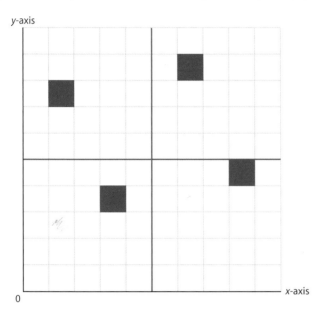

2 The white triangle is a reflection of the shaded triangle. Write down the co-ordinates of the white triangle.

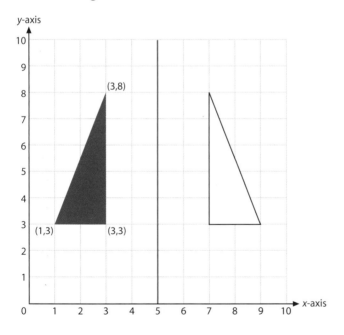

Aiming higher

1 Here are two regular hexagons.

a) Copy and shade two triangles to give a hexagon with just one line of symmetry.

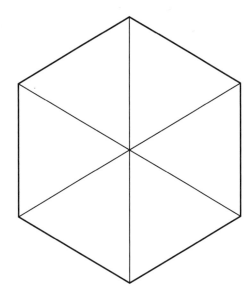

b) Copy and shade two triangles to give a hexagon with two lines of symmetry.

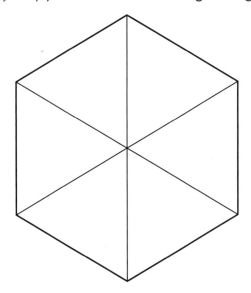

2   Here is a shaded square on a grid. Copy and shade in three more squares so that the design is symmetrical in both mirror lines.

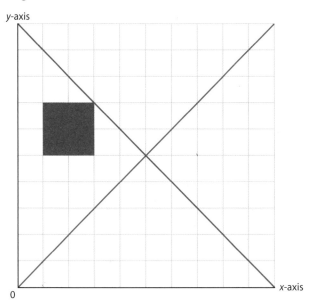

Using and applying

1   Explain how to translate shape A so that it covers shape B.

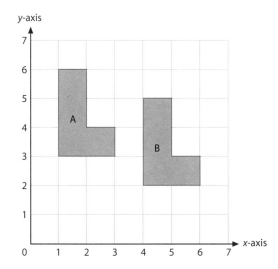

17 Estimating and drawing angles

What will you learn?

How to estimate, draw and measure acute and obtuse angles using an angle measurer or protractor and how to calculate angles in a straight line

I know how to:

- draw lines accurately
- read the scale on a protractor or angle measurer.

I need to be able to:

- recognise acute, obtuse and right angles.

Example

Which of these angles are acute and which are obtuse? Estimate the size of each angle and then measure each angle.

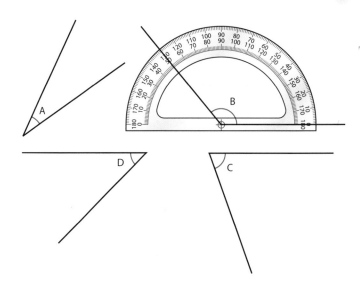

- *Acute are A, C, D; obtuse is B.*
- *A is 30°   B is 130°   C is 70°   D is 45°*

Key facts

Acute angles are less than 90°; obtuse angles are greater than 90° and less than 180°.
Angles on a straight line add up to 180°.

Language

Acute angles   are less than 90°

Obtuse angles   are greater than 90° and less than 180°

On track

1 This is a six-sided star.

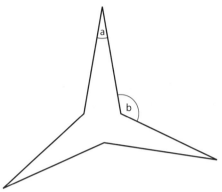

Measure angles **a** and **b** accurately.

2 **RS** is a straight line.

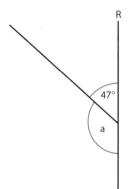

Calculate the size of
angle **a**.

Aiming higher

1 Copy and complete the table below about the angles in
the star.

Put a tick in the correct box depending on whether the angle is
acute or obtuse.

Estimate, in degrees, the size of each angle and then measure
the angles.

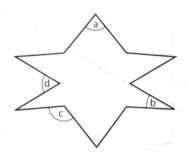

Angle	Acute angle	Obtuse angle	Estimate of size in degrees	Actual size in degrees
a	✓			80
b	✓			
c		✓		
d	✓		65	

Using and applying

1 **AB** is a straight line.

Calculate the size of angle **x**.

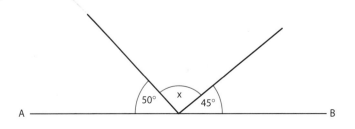

18 Length, weight and capacity with metric units

What will you learn?

How to read, choose, use and record standard metric units to estimate and measure length, weight and capacity to a suitable degree of accuracy, how to convert larger to smaller units using decimals to one place (e.g. change 2.6 kg to 2600 g) and how to measure weight using appropriate measuring instruments and state measurements in kilograms and grams

I know how to:

● multiply and divide by 10, 100, etc.

I need to be able to:

● read scales on measuring instruments accurately

● measure accurately

● change from mm to cm or from cm to m, etc.

Example

Choose the best instrument in the box to make each of the measurements below. Write down your estimate for each measure.

metre rule	30-cm ruler	kitchen scales	bathroom scales
kitchen measuring jug		teaspoon	

Height of a classroom   Dose of cough medicine

Weight of a suitcase   Weight of a potato

● *Metre rule – about 2.5 m*   ● *Teaspoon – 5 ml (0.005 l)*

● *Bathroom scales – about 20 kg*   ● *Kitchen scales – about 200 g (0.2 kg)*

Key facts

10 mm in 1 cm   100 cm in 1 m   1000 m in 1 km   1000 g in 1 kg   1000 ml in 1 *l*

Language

centi ... in measurement 'centi' means a hundredth. For example, centimetre is a hundredth of a metre

kilo ... in measurement 'kilo' means a thousand. For example, kilometre is a thousand metres

On track

1 **a)** Write 26.5 kg in grams.   **b)** Write 7 kg 300 g as a decimal.

2 How many glasses each holding 150 ml can be filled from this jug of orange juice?

3 Choose the most suitable measurement from the box to complete the sentences below.

2 mm	2 m	2 cm	2 l	2 km	10 m	10 g	10 kg	250 ml	2.5 l

a) A match stick is about … thick.

b) The capacity of a mug is about …

c) The weight of a 5p piece is about …

d) The height of most doors is about …

e) A bus is about … long.

 Aiming higher

1 A tin of rice pudding weighs 425 g. How many grams less than 1 kg is this?

2 Put these lengths in order, the shortest first: $\frac{1}{2}$ m   1.2 km   3 cm   25 mm

 Using and applying

1 **a)** Which measurement is equivalent to 1.3 l?

130 ml   1003 ml   1300 ml   103 ml?

How do you know?

b) Which of these measurements is equivalent to 2.07 m?

270 cm   2007 cm   207 cm   270 cm

How did you know?

2 This earring is made from gold wire. Measure accurately the total length of gold wire in the earring.

Give the units of your answer.

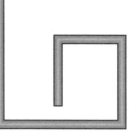

19 Reading scales

What will you learn?

How to interpret a reading that lies between two unnumbered divisions on a scale and how to find the value of each interval on a scale so that measurements can be read accurately

I know how to:

● change between grams and kilograms, millilitres and litres.

I need to be able to:

● read scales on measuring instruments accurately.

Example

What is the distance between the two small arrows on the scale?

The long arrow marks the end of a piece of wood.

How many centimetres short of a metre is this piece of wood?

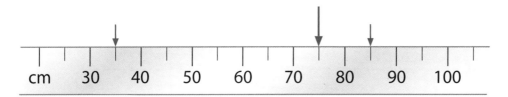

● *Distance = 50 cm*

● *The wood is 100 cm – 75 cm = 25 cm short*

Key fact

The measurements on scales can be very different. You will need to remember, for example, that there are 1000 g in a kilogram and 1000 ml in a litre. You will need to count the divisions between the scales to decide on the values between the marks that are labelled.

Language

Interval   the name given to the space between two divisions on a scale

On track

1 150 ml of water are poured out from this container.

How much water is left in the container?

2 100 ml of water are added to the water in this container.

Copy and draw a line to show the new level of the water in the

container. Write down what the new reading would be.

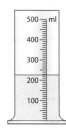

Aiming higher

1 Estimate the readings on these scales.

Use the units in your answers.

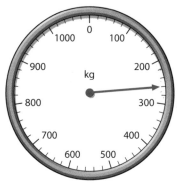

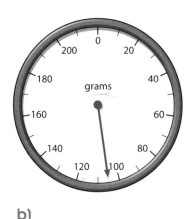

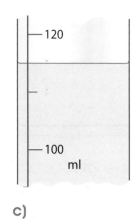

a)   b)   c)

2 This is the scale on a car's speedometer.

The speed limit is 50 miles per hour.

About how many miles per hour is the car above the speed limit?

Using and applying

1 A piece of cheese has a mass of 850 g. Draw a scale like the one below and mark

an arrow on it to show the reading for 850 g.

| 0 | 500 g | 1 kg | 1500 g | 2 kg |

How did you know where to draw the arrow?

20 Area and perimeter

What will you learn?

How to draw and measure lines to the nearest millimetre, calculate the perimeter of a shape and use the formula to work out the area of a rectangle

I know how to:

● calculate with numbers with one decimal place.

I need to be able to:

● distinguish between perimeter and area.

Example

Find the area of a rectangle with length 8.2 cm and width of 5.2 cm.

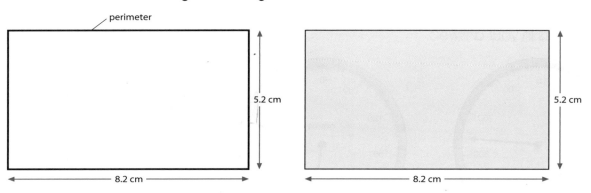

perimeter

5.2 cm

5.2 cm

8.2 cm

8.2 cm

● *Area is length × width = 8.2 × 5.2 = 42.64 cm²*
● *Perimeter is 8.2 + 5.2 + 8.2 + 5.2 = 26.8 cm*

Key facts

The perimeter of a rectangle is its length + width + length + width. The units are centimetres or metres, etc.
The area of a rectangle is its length × width. The units are cm² or m², etc.

Language

Perimeter   the perimeter of a rectangle is its length + width + length + width or 2 × length + 2 × width
The units are centimetres or metres or kilometres, etc. (units of length)
Area   the amount of space covered by a shape
Equilateral   usually an equilateral triangle – all the sides have the same length

On track

1. What is the perimeter of:

a) a regular octagon with sides of 35 mm?

b) An equilateral triangle with sides of 9.6 cm?

2. A square has a perimeter of 96 cm. How long is each side?

3. What is the perimeter and area of a rectangle with length 11 m and width 4 m?

Aiming higher

1. What is the area of a rectangle measuring 43 cm by 34 cm?

2. The area of a rectangle is 132 m^2. The shortest side is 6 m long. What is the length of the longest side?

3. An equilateral triangle is drawn on one side of a square with a side length of 9.4 cm. Calculate the perimeter of the shape that is made.

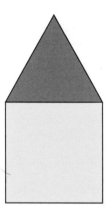

Using and applying

1. A rectangle has a perimeter of 42 m. The shortest side is 8 m long. What is the length of the longest side? How did you work it out?

2. The area of a rectangle is 24 cm². What are the lengths of the sides? Are there other possible answers?

3. a) Calculate the area and perimeter of rectangle A with length 4 cm and width 3 cm.

b) Calculate the area and perimeter of rectangle B with length 5 cm and width 4 cm. What do you notice about the areas and perimeters?

c) Can you find a rectangle where the perimeter and area only differ by 1?

21 Timetables and time

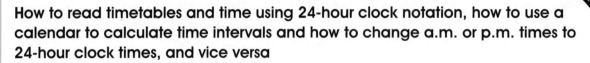

What will you learn?

How to read timetables and time using 24-hour clock notation, how to use a calendar to calculate time intervals and how to change a.m. or p.m. times to 24-hour clock times, and vice versa

I know how to:

● tell the time using the 24-hour clock.

I need to be able to:

● change the time from and to the 24-hour clock

● read a calendar.

Example

Here is part of a train timetable.

Edinburgh	–	09:35	–	–	13:35	–
Glasgow	09:15	–	11:15	13:15	–	13:45
Stirling	09:57	–	11:57	13:57	–	14:29
Perth	10:34	10:51	12:34	14:34	14:50	15:15
Inverness	–	13:10	–	–	17:05	–

How long does the first train from Glasgow to Perth take to travel?

Ellen is at Edinburgh station at 1:30 p.m. She wants to travel to Inverness. She catches the next train. At what time will she arrive in Inverness?

● *1 hour 19 minutes.*

● *17:05.*

Key facts

a.m. is the time before 12 noon (midday); p.m. is the time from noon until midnight. In the 24-hour clock, time is given using four digits. For example, 07:05 for five past seven in the morning; or 17:10 for ten past five in the afternoon.

Language

See the **Key facts** for definitions of a.m. and p.m. and the 24-hour clock

On track

1 Here is the calendar for September 2007.

	September				
M		3	10	17	24
T		4	11	18	25
W		5	12	19	26
T		6	13	20	27
F		7	14	21	28
S	1	8	15	22	29
S	2	9	16	23	30

a) Kathy's birthday is on 23rd September. She has a party on the Saturday after her birthday. What date is this?

b) Janet's birthday is on 27th September. What day of the week is this?

c) School starts on the first Monday in September. What date is this?

2 How would the time twenty minutes past six in the evening be shown on a 24-hour digital clock?

Aiming higher

1 Here is part of a timetable.

Newcastle	07:44	08:24	09:35	09:40	10:26
York	08:44	09:27	10:34	10:44	11:27
Leeds	09:10			11:10	
Wakefield	09:23			11:23	
Sheffield	09:53	10:23	11:23	11:53	12:23
Derby	10:24	10:57	11:57	12:24	12:57

a) Which train travels from Newcastle to York in the shortest time? And how long does it take?

b) Emma arrives at Newcastle station five minutes after the 07:44 train has left. She wants to go to Wakefield. How much longer does she have to wait for the next train?

2 The time on Simon's digital watch is 18:02. Simon's watch is seven minutes fast. How should the correct time be displayed?

Using and applying

1 A plane takes off on Wednesday at 22:57. It lands on Thursday at 06:05. How long is the flight in hours and minutes? Show how you calculated your answer.

22 Simple probability

What will you learn?

How to describe how likely an event is to happen using the language of chance or likelihood, and how to justify a statement

I know how to:

● read a probability scale.

I need to be able to:

● justify or explain my reasoning.

Example

Here is a spinner that is a regular octagon.

Write 1, 2 or 3 in each section of the spinner so that 1 and 3 are equally likely to come up and 2 is the least likely to come up.

● *There are eight spaces for numbers. 1 and 3 are equally likely so must take 3 spaces each leaving two spaces for 2. If there was only one space with 2 in it, then either 1 or 3 would have more spaces and then the two numbers wouldn't be equally likely.*

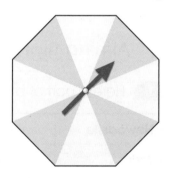

Key fact

The chance of something happening is measured by reference to a scale – see 'scale' in **Language** below.

Language

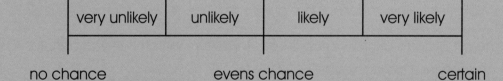

very unlikely	unlikely	likely	very likely

no chance   evens chance   certain

Likely and **unlikely**, **certain** and **no chance** words that are used to describe the likelihood of something happening. The simple way of understanding what they mean is to look at a scale. At one end there is 'no chance' – it won't happen; at the other end something is sure to happen – it is 'certain'. In between, the scale moves from unlikely to likely passing through a middle point where the chances are 'even'

On track

1   1 When you roll a normal dice, how likely are you to roll a number bigger than 2?
Use the language of the probability scale to give your answer.

Aiming higher

1   James throws a normal six-sided dice.

Choose the best word from the box to complete each of the sentences below.

| certain | very likely | likely | unlikely | very unlikely | impossible |

a) It is … that James will get a number less than seven.

b) It is … that James will get a six.

c) It is … that James will get a two.

d) It is … that James will get a number bigger than six.

e) It is … that James will get a number bigger than one.

Using and applying

1   Here is a net for a dice. Label each side
so that rolling an even number is very unlikely.

2   Here is a square spinner.

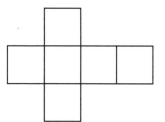

Look at the statements below.

For each one put a tick (✓) if it is correct.

Put a cross (✗) if it is not correct.

'1' is the most likely score.	
'2' and '4' are equally likely scores.	
There is an evens chance of an odd number score	
A score of '3' or more is as likely as a score of less than '3'.	

23 Selecting and collecting data

What will you learn?

How to decide what information needs to be collected to answer a question and how best to collect it, and how to explain what a table, graph or chart tells us

I know how to:

● read the scales on graphs, etc.

I need to be able to:

● consider further questions that a table or graph raises.

Example

Class 6 count how many seeds they find under two different trees. They show the data in a graph.

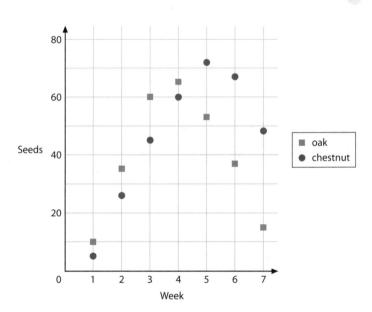

What questions could you ask about the data in this graph?

● *Examples could be: Which tree produced most seeds? How many seeds were found in week 3? How many seeds were found altogether over the seven weeks?*

Key fact

Graphs are useful to compare sets of data.

Language

Bar chart   see question 1 in **Using and applying** for example
Pie chart   see question 2 in **On track** for example
Graph   see the question in the **Example** above

On track

1 How could you find out:

a) what types of pet are owned by the children in your class?

b) what is their favourite type of music?

2 This pie chart shows the lunch choices of Year 6 children at a school.

28 children in Year 6 go home for lunch.

What questions could you ask and answer from this pie chart?

Write down three questions and answer them.

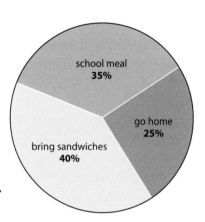

Aiming higher

1 This pie chart shows how the children in Classes 6A and 6B best like their potatoes cooked.

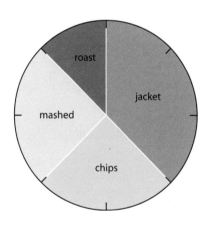

What questions could you ask about this data?

Using and applying

1 This graph shows the distances some children jumped.

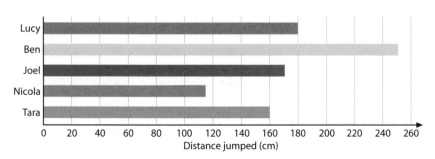

Write down three questions about this data and then answer them.

24 Frequency tables, pictograms and bar charts

What will you learn?

How to construct frequency tables, pictograms and bar and line graphs to represent the frequencies of events and changes over time

I know how to:

● read scales on graphs and frequency tables.

I need to be able to:

● explain why I chose to represent data using a particular table, graph or chart.

Example

For one week a dentist made a survey of the number of fillings his patients had who came into his surgery. The table shows the results.

0	2	1	2	1	1	2	3	1	0	2	3
1	2	1	3	0	3	1	2	0	0	2	0
2	0	1	2	3	1	4	2	1	4	1	

Draw a tally chart to show this data.

Draw a graph to show the data. What sort of graph will you choose?

● *A bar chart or a stick chart (a bar line graph) would be appropriate here.*

Number of fillings	Frequency
0	卅 //
1	卅 卅 /
2	卅 卅
3	卅
4	//

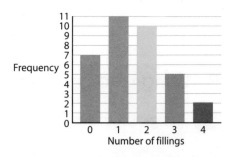

Key fact

You must have equal intervals along each scale.

Language

You need to be able to identify the different graphs:

bar chart; pie chart; tally chart

On track

1 Some children measured the heights of trees in a wood. The pictogram below shows their results.

Height	Number of trees
Up to 10 m	🌳🌳🌳🌳🌳
Between 10m and 20m	🌳🌳🌳🌳🌳🌳🌲

🌳 represents 4 trees

a) How many trees were up to 10m tall?

b) How many trees were between 10m and 20m tall?

c) There were 34 trees between 20m and 30m tall. Draw a pictogram to show this.

Aiming higher

1 This bar chart shows the total number of goals scored in each first-round match of the World Cup in Germany in 2006.

a) In how many matches were no goals scored?

b) In how many matches were less than three goals scored?

c) How many matches were played in the first round of the World Cup in Germany in 2006?

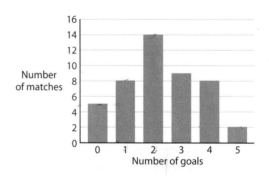

Using and applying

1 Amy has invented a dice game. It involves throwing two normal dice.

A person's score is the higher of the two numbers showing.

The score here is 5.

The score here is 3.

This bar line chart shows the scores Amy found after some throws.

a) Which score was the least frequent?

b) What was the total number of times Amy threw the two dice?

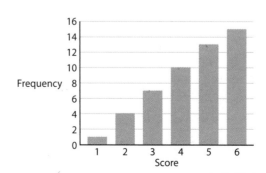

25 Finding the mode

What will you learn?

How to find and interpret the mode of a set of data

I know how to:

● read tables.

I need to be able to:

● put numbers in order of size.

Example

Find the mode of these numbers:

1   5   2   4   8   3   1

● *It helps to rewrite the numbers in order:*

1   1   2   3   4   5   8

The mode is 1.

Key facts

It helps to rewrite the numbers in a set of data in order, from smallest to largest or largest to smallest.
There can be more than one mode.

Language

The mode   the most common value or piece of information in a set of data

 ## On track

1 Write a number in each of these boxes so that the mode of the five numbers is 8.

2 The marks scored by 16 boys in a test were as follows:

20	16	18	17	16	18	14	13
18	18	15	18	19	9	12	13

Find the mode of the number of marks scored.

Aiming higher

1 The ages of a group of people are as follows:

19   23   53   19   16   26   77   19   27

Find the modal age.

2 Here is a list of the weights of people in a 'Keep Fit' class.

73 kg   58 kg   61 kg   43 kg   81 kg   53 kg   73 kg   70 kg   62 kg

Find the modal weight.

Using and applying

1 Here are the ages of some 1p coins collected in a survey.

0 years old means that a coin was dated 2007.

0	0	1	1	1	2	2	2	2	2
2	3	3	3	3	4	4	5	5	5
6	6	7	7	7	8	9	10	10	10

a) What is the mode of the ages of these coins?

b) In another survey with 2p coins, the mode was 5 years. Again 0 years old means that a coin was dated 2007.

Explain what this means in everyday language.

2 These are the marks for a tables test.

Aaron	20	Daya	15	Jabeen	15	Rabia	18
Ainesh	15	Devak	18	James	18	Raja	14
Amy	17	Habiba	20	Jeeval	14	Robert	20
Barbara	19	Haridas	18	Jennifer	19	Shirley	18
Caesar	14	Harini	17	John	15	Tom	19
Chris	15	Helli	15	Lalan	17	Wasan	15
David	17	Indira	12	Mary	13	William	10

Amy says that just over half the class got more than the mode mark.

Is she right?

Explain how you know.

26 Exploring patterns and relationships

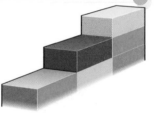

What will you learn?

How to explore patterns, properties and relationships, how to make a general statement involving numbers or shapes and identify examples for which the statement is true or false

I know how to:

● work out the differences between numbers in a sequence.

I need to be able to:

● explain how I sorted numbers and shapes.

Example

Neta is playing with some building bricks. She stacks up the bricks so that each row has one less brick than the row below.

Neta has a total of 55 bricks.

She wants to end up with one brick on top.

How many bricks should she put in the bottom row?

● *It is probably easier to start at the top and work down the stack counting the number of bricks and putting the totals in a table.*

Row	1	2	3	4	5	6	7	8	9	10
Number of bricks	1	2	3	4	5	6	7	8	9	10
Total	1	3	6	10	15	21	28	36	45	55

So Neta needs ten bricks in the bottom row.

Key fact

A sequence will have the same difference between each term.

Language

Sequences and patterns arrangements of numbers or shapes that change by the same amount through the arrangement

 On track

1 Explore this pattern of grey and white squares.

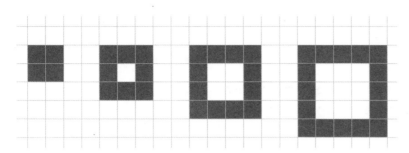

Write down two facts about the number of grey squares in each part of the pattern.

2 Here are some shapes in groups.

  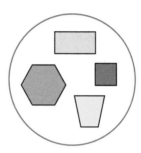

a) Write down a property of all the shapes in:

(i) A   **(ii)** B   **(iii)** C

b) Here is another shape. Should it go into A, B or C or does it not fit anywhere?

Explain your answer.

 Aiming higher

1 Look at these four numbers.

    4   5   25   32

Think of a property that is true for two of them and false for the other two numbers. Now think of some different properties.

Using and applying

1 Here is a pattern of dots.

a) Copy and draw the next pattern in the sequence, and copy and complete the table.

Pattern number	1	2	3	4	5	10
Number of dots	2	4	6	8		

b) Explain, without drawing, how you worked out the number of dots in the tenth pattern.

c) James says 'The number of dots in any of the pattern numbers here is always even.'

Is he right? If so can you explain why?

2 Here is a pattern of dots.

a) Copy and draw the next pattern in the sequence, and copy and complete the table.

Pattern number	1	2	3	4	5	10
Number of dots	3	6				

b) Explain, without drawing, how you worked out the number of dots in the tenth pattern.

3 Here is a pattern of dots.

a) Copy and draw the next pattern in the sequence, and copy and complete the table.

Pattern number	1	2	3	4	5	10
Number of dots	1	3	5	7		

b) Explain, without drawing, how you worked out the number of dots in the tenth pattern.

c) 'The numbers of dots is always odd.' Is this true? Explain.